UNFETTERED IMAGINATION

(A Place of Thoughts, Musings and Quotes)

Published by

Unfettered Imagination

Edited by Mobani Biswas

Published by : Poetry World Org.

Publisher's Address : Haryana

Printed under PWO in India

 Special credits to Tanishi, Pragya Sankhala, Dr.Niveditha and Dr.Nitin chopra.

Edition : I (2021)

ISBN (Paperback) - 9789390724734

Book Design by POETRY WORLD

UNFETTERED IMAGINATION

(A Place of Thoughts, Musings and Quotes)

Compiled And Edited By

Mobani Biswas

A girl who believes in penning pieces out of unexpressed emotions, Mobani started writing poems at the age of 13. Science didn't interest her after 12th grade and she found her true calling in the folds of literature.

Author of the book, ***Window to the World***, Mobani believes without words the world would be a dreary place to live in. After completing her B.A. (Hons.) in English literature from Delhi University she pursued Masters in English Literature from the University of Allahabad, after completing B.Ed., she aims to teach and share her knowledge with the children who are the future of our country.

Instagram Id- painting_through_words

Facebook Page- Thoughts' Cauldron

E-mail: mobani.biswas@gmail.com

PREFACE

In life's hustle-bustle, there comes a time when our diary becomes our friend, a place where we can pour our emotions, not necessarily in the form of poems or long stories. Somewhere in the corner of our heart lurks a writer, which many times die in the folds of the diaries because those thoughts or emotions never get a chance to see the light of the day.

Words are beautiful, and when they are used to express some unsaid things, then their beauty increases all the more.

Through this book we make a small attempt to bring those thoughts and those writers to the forefront. Those ideas and musings that may have died in the pages of the diaries are now immortalized in a book.

This is what the beauty of this book is all about.

We bring you a bouquet of beautiful emotions compiled together like a gorgeous garland, to beautify your reading experience.

INDEX

THE FIRST TIME WE MET....11
BEING HUMAN....12
EVOCATIONS OF YOURS....13
I SHALL WAIT FOR YOU....14
PARADOXICAL LOVE....15
ALWAYS WANTED TO TELL YOU....16
SHE IS ONE OF A KIND....17
I WISH I COULD....18
LAST NIGHT....19
UNRAVELLED WITHIN....20
LIFE....21
PEOPLE ARE LIKE......22
THE LETTER....23
LOST....24
COME, MY BELOVED!....25
HOPE....26
SOUL....27
FILTER....28
RESPECT HIM....29
DEAR DESTINY....30
ALONE....31
BEING YOURSELF....32
RAIN....33

WINTER 34
MOVE ON 35
HOPE 36
MAYBE 37
CREATOR 38
THE HEART 39
STARING AT THE CEILING 40
HAPPINESS 41
ELIXIR 42
ADIEU! 43
SUNRISE 44
ADULTING 45
REST BUT DON'T QUIT 46
LOVE YOURSELF 47
LIVING IN HEAVEN 48
RISKY REWARD 49
CHAOS AND PEACE 50
A CALL AWAY 51
LIFE QUOTES 52
YOU 53

“

THE FIRST TIME WE MET

The first time we met-

When I first saw you,

I was a little afraid to meet you,

I could not help but stare at you,

How eventually we started skipping sleep,

Just to listen to each other breathe.

Aakanksha Srivastava

”

“

BEING HUMAN

Look, everything's here is burning inside,

Oh! Yes, being a human is fragile.

All of it suffocates me until I cried,

Why it's so hard here to survive?

I just want someone to be by my side,

one who feels proud to have me in life.

Aastha Zindagi

”

“

EVOCATIONS OF YOURS

My eyes reflect,

evocation of yours,

just have a glimpse in it,

the deeper you will go,

the more tragedy

you will come to know!

Aayesha Sarkare

”

“

I SHALL WAIT FOR YOU

I shall wait here, at the top of,

the pyramid of sedimentary emotions of love,

For you, like a myth-

Within this realistic campus of logic.

My solitariness travelling across the star-lit sky,

Searches for your intimate-absolute-embrace.

Abhishek Dutta Chowdhury

”

“

PARADOXICAL LOVE

I paint the turbid memories
With somber rays of hope and light
But your calmness break my veins to swamp with blue
Scribbling words that define you
The poetry in my eyes is an institution of emotions
With verses soaked in tears
I bathe in a river of questions
Is it an empty dream or mere fantasy?
That your love feels so paradoxical to me
Your love doesn’t shackle my wings
In this materialistic world
It doesn’t confine me like a treasure by the fireside
It vents my ocean of feelings that I try to stay
It lights my night with ambrosial stars
And fills my day with ostentatious display
It gives me flames of intimacy and firmness
To set my soul free in a phase of intransigence
Like the blooming of recalcitrant wildflower with beauty
and grandeur

Alisha Khwaja

”

“

ALWAYS WANTED TO TELL YOU

Maybe this is what my eyes
always wanted to tell you…

Not only my love but,
all the pain in my heart...

Sneaking out of my eyes, it tries to show you...

The more I missed you, the more I love you...

Ankita Singh

”

“

SHE IS ONE OF A KIND

"They definitely should pay for the things they did to me"

She said.

"They no longer have you in their lives,

Isn't that punishment enough"

He smiled.

Indeed no one would ever want to lose
such a person like her.

Arvind Raj K

”

“

I WISH I COULD

I wish we could chatter all night,

I wish everything to get right,

I wish to have those minutes of talk,

School to our ways, when we used to walk,

But until I'm restrained from this gain,

I wish I could dream again!

Aryan Mishra

”

“

LAST NIGHT

She woke up to the creased bed sheets,

reminding her of his smell

Crumbled jeans on the floor, reminding her of his hips.

Empty beer cans, reminding her of his lips.

Making her crave and falling for more!

Athira Muralidharan

”

“

UNRAVELLED WITHIN

The heart pounded and sadness surrounded me.

Inside the volcano erupted.

But the lips were sealed,

Though the eyes did speak.

Was it still there within?

Or was it just a memory in a spin?

Batul Tasneem

”

“

LIFE

Life is a constant loop of

WHAT IFs and I WISH

and in between

We've got some moments to cherish

Harshita Hardiya

”

PEOPLE ARE LIKE...

People are like leaves,

When you're fresh and new

they stay with you,

When you are down and dry

all alone you lie.

Kalaivani Umapathy

“

THE LETTER

Nothing could make me feel better until I wrote a letter.
A letter to myself, which reiterated that it is okay to be not okay.

The letter made me feel better because it made me forget all
those letters which brought bitter memories!
Because it made me not to look at the
Doors which I closed for all reasons.
Because it made me look at the mirror
And embrace my curves which I hated for no reasons.
Because the letter made me forgive myself for all the mistakes.
Because the letter made me love my flowers and thorns in the same way.

It reiterated why I took so long to write it down.
When to build boundaries; When to cross boundaries
How to get my pieces back in a different, yet in the most beautiful way.

Nothing could make me feel better until I wrote a letter.
A letter to myself, which reiterated that
It is okay to be not okay.

Kavya Das

”

“

LOST

Lost, hoping to be found again, a hope to set myself right again.

The thoughts, the will, the animation, lost...

Lost between that fragile line of accomplishment & disappointment.

Lost in the array of disarray, in the shower of truths not spoken.

Lost too deep in the chaos to call out again.

Lost... yet hoping to be found again.

Maanas Bhadauria

”

“

COME, MY BELOVED!

Come my beloved, come to me.

My heart awaits you like a Majnun desperate.

You're the hue of my rusty blood,

Of my withered autumn leaves,

Of my gasping heart that bleeds through

the corner of my hooded eyes.

Madiha Tariq

”

“

HOPE

I was in hope,

Hoping better is on its way

But I was unaware that things

were actually getting away..

Mansi Jawale

”

“

SOUL

It knows

the truth of your lies.

A poet’s muse,

Immortal in existence.

A four-letter word sums it up-

‘SOUL’

Mobani Biswas

”

“

FILTER

No filter can help you look beautiful.

until you’re not happy from inside.

When you’re really happy,

you don't require any filter to look beautiful.

ÑëHå Sharma

”

“

RESPECT HIM

When your competitor wins over you, respect him

because he is your master.

When you win over your competitor, respect him

because he can be your master in future.

Don't underestimate anyone.

Nivetha R C

”

“

DEAR DESTINY

I wish I could tell you how much I love you...
I wish I could tell you how much I longed for you…
I wish I could tell you; I wanted that old us back…
But why?
Why did we tear apart?
Why did we part our ways?
Why were all my dreams of love left incomplete? And
many more questions in my head...
Waiting to be answered by you...
Dear destiny,
Could you please help us meet
At least once

Pratyusha Dasari

”

“

ALONE

Alone you are, move ahead,

the path you follow is full of threat,

Overlook and see straight,

When vision is clear, get blind for the rest,

Paint your aim on a clean slate,

Sharpen your weapons, and begin your journey,

before it gets too late.

Puja Parashar

”

“

BEING YOURSELF

Being yourself and being bold is when
you accept yourself as you are,
and when you are bold enough
to present yourself as you are
with a blend of scars, scratches,
hurts, and a smile.

R.Susanna Celsia

”

“

RAIN

We live in a polluted shell,

no one can clean her up.

Keep dreaming if not keen to wake up to a nightmare

It should just pour,

But keep in mind

It doesn't rain forever,

No mist will lay in the atmosphere forever

and no thunder shall strike forever.

Reatile Brian Molefe

”

“

WINTER

Singing birds of spring.

Touch of warm midsummer wind.

Fall of autumn arrived.

But you never stayed

to watch winter snow with me beside.

Rida Fatima

”

“

MOVE ON

She was smiling again.

But this time

not for anyone else but,

for herself.

Ronak Parveen

”

"

HOPE

Hold onto that spark of hope

which has the capability

to reform the light in your

heart once faded by darkness.

S.Suganthi

"

“

MAYBE

And maybe, just maybe,
we will find each other again when the time will be right
and we both will be mature enough.
When we have set our careers
and know what is right for us.
Then maybe we can start over again and talk about things
we have already talked about.
Play games we have already played.
Relearn things we already know and
fall in love with each other again.

Shivangi Jain

”

“

CREATOR

Either creation

creates the creator

or creator creates

the creation.

Shreyash

”

“

THE HEART

Many secrets are buried deep in this heart,

Yes, many secrets are buried in this heart,

It’s difficult, but a smile plays on my lips from the start,

This heart is under a lot of pain but still,

I have kept my tears hidden from this world's game.

Shoaib Aalam

”

“

STARING AT THE CEILING

Late at night, lost in clouded thoughts,

Analyzing endlessly, trying to join the dots...

As I worry about everything I might lack,

I stare at the ceiling and it stares back...

Completely plain, black and peacefully flat,

I sometimes wish I could feel like that...

Shrija Mukherjee

”

“

HAPPINESS

Wondering and waiting to drench in the bright light of happiness,

As happiness is not always gained by flying up in the bright sky,

But also by yielding and watching an inspiring flower to grow in the mud!

The true happiness always comes with love and care,

And the worth of this happiness should be honoured with delightful glory!

Sonal Torane

”

“

ELIXIR

Dejection had suddenly become a way of life.
Waking up was a task.
My eyelids often gave up on me, refusing to open.
The sunshine felt like a friend who I knew once upon a time, but never bothered to check in.
It felt like the miners had successfully made a huge pit,
In my stomach.
They kept digging though, never stopped.
Shoulders kept drooping,
My spine rebelled and never stayed erect.
Every Monday, I'd sit in her office, tell her the same things.
There was never anything different to offer.
Sometimes I felt I should make up a story about how I feel,
At least one of us will be amused.
I was numb, not a single emotion could be felt.
It felt like slow paralysis. Slow but deathly.
Every night I'd stare at the bottle sitting next to my lamp.
With cold hands I would try to pick it up but, would instantly put it back.
One night, I picked it up, gulped it down, in one shot.
It felt like elixir, An out of body experience,
The only difference being,
I would never get a chance to come back into this body.

Stoic

”

“

ADIEU!

I was dying in you,

Drowning without a clue!

Many fathoms deep, yet I continue,

To fall for everything that's untrue.

Plenty of hues yet your wings chose

the darkest of blue to fly over my residue.

My heart depreciates yet the pain renews,

To know only thing I couldn't do is to bid you Adieu!

Suvaiba Zaheen

”

“

SUNRISE

Situations in life,

are not the same everywhere

Just like the sunset,

there is a sunrise somewhere...!!

Titas Chakraborty

”

“

ADULTING

Trapped with head full of thoughts

wide awake in the midway of the night

Fighting with the inner demons

stumbling to deal with ourselves.

Thinking where we went wrong and

Making it difficult to show up

if this adulting is not a real mess

then what it is?

Uja Sowndharya

”

“

REST BUT DON’T QUIT

If you’re tired, go for campfire

Go and sleep under the starlight sky

And wake up to the dancing tunes

Played by the cloud

Take rest but don't quit.

V. Sai Gayathri

”

“

LOVE YOURSELF

Do the work,

Try the hard things.

Feel the darkness,

Acknowledge your mistake,

then love yourself

again and again.

Vaibhav Trivedi

”

“

LIVING IN HEAVEN

Everything seemed to be working well,

Until we found that instead of heaven we were dragged to hell

Wronged it felt to live a life so upright.

Yet we could not see anything in sight.

Confused about the work we did all this while,

Until we saw ourselves hanging by a fan with smile.

Vaishnavi Gupta

”

“

RISKY REWARD

At night when silence seduces
I roam alone with dreams of you

whence comes an alluring whisper
of a stolen kiss from breathless lips

a risky reward to unite for evermore:
my soul in exchange for yours.

Vani A. Aethereal_Psyche

”

“

CHAOS AND PEACE

He heard those unheard screams,

He saw the pain others couldn't see,

He stood by me when no one else did,

When everyone blamed my demons, he saw the beauty in me.

In the world full of darkness, he became my peace.

Vanshika Singh

”

“

A CALL AWAY

My dear friend,

Are you still fighting the monsters?
the ‘no’ that took over
the ‘yes’ that faltered before,
do they still fight?
The gravity of gray clouds
that held you low,
Is it still winning over the sunshine?

Are you still walking?
Are you still picking up calls?

Are you doing okay?

Word Pirate (Sudeshna Das)

”

“

LIFE QUOTES

Trust everyone,

but with caution,

because sometimes

even one's own teeth

can bite the tongue..

Yash Milind Gosavi

”

“

YOU

Zero intention of letting you go.

As I look into your eyes I think,

May this smile never fade away.

A special bond we share.

Never change yourself and never give up.

Zainab Abid

”